CW00693065

A BOOK OF

DR R BRASCH

FRIENDSHIP

Angus&Robertson
An imprint of HarperCollins*Publishers*

To Faith and Don Fraser
two good friends

ACKNOWLEDGEMENTS

Scripture quotations are from The New King James Version,
Copyright © 1982 by Thomas Nelson Inc.
Used by permission.

Sincere thanks to the following author and publisher who kindly
granted permission to quote from their work:

Mr Russ Tyson, from his *Philosopher's Note Book*, 1961.

Harvard University Press, for Ralph Waldo Emerson's *Essays*, first series.
Faber and Faber, for Dag Hammarskjold's *Markings*.

All efforts have been made to contact the copyright owners of the
material in this book. Where this has not been possible, the Publishers
invite the persons concerned to contact them.

An Angus & Robertson Publication

Angus&Robertson, an imprint of
HarperCollins *Publishers*
25 Ryde Road, Pymble, Sydney NSW 2073, Australia
31 View Road, Glenfield, Auckland 10, New Zealand
77-85 Fulham Palace Road, London W6 8JB, United Kingdom
10 East 53rd Street, New York NY 10022, USA

First published in Australia in 1994

Copyright © Text R. Brasch 1994

National Library of Australia
Cataloguing-in-Publication data:

Brasch, R. (Rudolph), 1912-
A book of friendship
ISBN 0 207 18346 5.

1. Friendship - Literary collections. 2. Friendship - Quotations,
maxims, etc. I. Title.
808.80353

Border illustration by Karen Carter
Floral motifs by Megan Smith

Printed in Hong Kong

5 4 3 2 1
97 96 95 94

CONTENTS

INTRODUCTION

*A faithful friend
is the medicine of life*

APOCRYPHA

ONE OF THE most rewarding experiences in life is when you unexpectedly meet friends and their eyes light up with pleasure to see you.

Friendship is a precious and essential gift. We all need to have a friend, and to be a friend makes our lives so much more meaningful. This has applied to every generation, but no period in history has been in greater need of friendship than our present one, with its loss of personal relationships, mechanised communication and continuous rush. So many people in our urbanised society live isolated and lonely lives.

That is why I have written this book. It deals with every aspect of friendship and its all-important relevance. It tells how to make and keep friends and speaks of the qualities and pitfalls of friendship. We follow the various stages of friendship, from infancy to old age. Historic friendships are discussed and the traditional symbols of friendship are explained. Examples of the various features of friendship are given by way of poetry, proverbs and sayings, or as passed down to us in parables and fables. Also, since the realm of friendship extends beyond human relationships to include animals, an entire chapter is devoted to this subject.

In the pages that follow, I hope you will share with me the beauty of friendship and all it can add to your life.

Our need for friends

EVERYONE NEEDS FRIENDS. To have even a single friend can make all the difference in the world: it makes you feel that you are not alone, that at least someone cares and takes notice of your existence. Merely to know that a friend is near is a wonderful comfort and reassurance. This applies to all types of circumstances and life situations.

A telling example is that of Rupert Brooke, the celebrated English poet who, tragically, died so young during the Great War. When sailing to the United States in 1913, no one came to see him off, yet everyone else on board seemed to have a friend.

Looking down from the railings, Brooke noticed a grubby little urchin hanging about on the dockside. He rushed down the gangway and made his way straight to the lad. 'If I give you sixpence', he asked, 'will you wave me off when the boat is leaving?' The boy gladly agreed, and he kept the bargain. When the liner was moving away from the docks, that scruffy little boy was waving the poet off. In recalling the incident, Rupert Brooke said that it was the best sixpence he had ever spent.

Some people may be too shy to make friends, or, possessed by a false sense of independence, may be unable to do so. So they shut themselves away, shunning human contact. Their attitude might easily be misinterpreted as a disinclination on their part to mix and relate. Don't be misled: understand their difficulty and their need. Offer them your hand of friendship in any way you can.

A man, feeling utterly lonely and rejected, had lost all zest for living. Desperate, he decided to take his life by drowning himself in the city's river. On leaving his home, however, he had second thoughts and made one reservation. Should he meet someone, on the way, whose eyes caught his and who, in doing so, gave the slightest indication that he took notice of him, he would turn back. But only then. Thus he set out on what, most likely, was going to be his last walk ever . . .

The story ends here. But it raises a significant question which concerns you personally. Had he met you on the way, would he have turned back?

Friendship needs no words - it is solitude delivered from the anguish of loneliness.

DAG HAMMARSKJÖLD

A missile of friendship

Passing through the hospital grounds, a nurse came across a boy who was using a mirror to reflect the sun's rays up to a window on the fifth floor. She was about to stop him, but changed her mind when the boy explained the reason to her. It was not just a child's prank.

'Up there', the boy told her, 'I have a sick friend, but I am not permitted to go and see him. So I am sending him some rays of sunshine, for him to know that I am down here thinking of him. It will make him better!'

Overcoming an obstacle, his young mind had ingeniously found a way to express his friendship.

There are no circumstances ever that should stop you from helping a friend. There is always some means to do so.

Friendship needs no words.

The door of friendship

Some people are very deliberate in selecting friends. They have only one consideration: how to make use of those 'friends' and to gain by them.

This applied to an eminent public figure. He had risen to the very top of his profession, filling a great variety of prestigious positions. He had achieved this not by his own effort but by a clever scheme he had conceived early on in life.

Even at school he had fostered friendships with children of the rich and well known, and he continued this policy with his contemporaries at college, university and, later, at work. He had kept up contact with them, convinced that one day some of them at least would fill offices of influence and that then their 'friendship' would pay high dividends — to him. And his plan succeeded.

In retrospect, however, it was clear that none of these friendships was genuine. People saw through him, and his success in life — so unearned — was deservedly short-lived. He had abused one of the most precious gifts that come our way.

A famous artist had been working on a painting for many years. Finally completed, it was ready to be unveiled in the gallery which had acquired it. A large expectant crowd had assembled, including representatives of the media. Television cameras were focused on the painting, which was still behind a curtain.

No sooner had the curator drawn the cord, when a hushed silence fell upon the gathering. The picture represented a door. But, it seemed unfinished! Where was the door handle? All eyes fell on the artist, waiting for an explanation.

'Friends', he said, 'you want to know where the handle is. The work *is* complete, for this is not an ordinary door. It is the door of friendship. Friendship must not be used as a "handle" to open doors to advancement, to the right connection or to unmerited gains!'

A selfless friendship alone is genuine and lasting. The quickest way to wipe out a friendship is to sponge on it.

Friendship must be for all times. One's friends are not merely here to comfort us in bad times. In good times we must share with them our happiness, our good news and our laughter. It is a strange person indeed, who can rejoice by himself or herself.

Instant friendship

THERE IS A great paradox in our modern world, with its urbanisation and huge blocks of apartment dwellings. At no time previously have more people lived so closely together, and yet been so far apart. Once doors were left unlocked. Now, living in constant fear, we install safety grilles and secure our homes with electronic gadgetry.

It is no wonder, therefore, that with so little communication, friendships of consequence have become rare. The majority of human relationships are merely superficial, restricted to games of cards, cocktail parties and occasional 'neighbourly' barbecues. Like the proverbial ships that pass in the night, we lack anchorage.

Still, there is no need to be friendless, provided *you* take the initiative. For instance, why don't you invite an acquaintance to visit you? You might be surprised to find how many interests, thoughts and concerns you share. In no time you will become friends. C. S. Lewis once observed that a friendship may start with the simple remark, 'What? You too! I thought I was the only one.'

A lady who lived all on her own had been good friends for many years with her next door neighbours. She dreaded the thought of what would happen when they moved away. When they did move, however, she was determined to make friends with the new people who were to occupy their former home. On the very day they arrived, she went across to welcome them.

'You must be tired and in need of a break — would you like to come to my place for a brief rest and a cup of tea?' she said. Her approach made the new neighbours feel at home straight away and they instantly became friends. We should all realise how important it is to be responsive rather than detached in human relationships.

If I am not for myself, who will be for me?
But if I am only for myself what am I?
And if not now, when?

Ethics of the Fathers

The touch of a hand

VISITING A JEWELLER friend's workshop, a woman admired the great variety of gems laid out on trays, sparkling and beautiful. However, she could not fail to notice among them one stone which seemed not to fit in. It was conspicuous — by its dullness.

Being an outspoken person, she immediately remarked on it. Her friend, without saying a word, picked up the stone and held it in his cupped hand for a short while. He then put it back onto the tray, where it outshone all the other gems, with fiery flashes of gold, red and green.

'What happened to it?' asked the intrigued visitor.

The jeweller explained the phenomenon. 'You see, this is an opal. In the trade it is known as a "sympathetic" jewel. Left on its own it appears insignificant — but a little warmth brings out all its glorious beauty. It was easy for me to do so by merely exposing the opal to the warmth of my hand.'

People are so often unhappy because they are left out in the cold. We all need the human touch — and the warmth of friendship.

To love and be loved is to feel the sun from both sides.
When friends meet, hearts warm.

When the fog lifts

A MAN WAS crossing a field in dense fog when he noticed a figure shrouded in the thick mist coming towards him. He was greatly frightened, for it looked like some ominous creature. However, as it came closer, he realised that it was a human. Getting nearer still, he recognised him — it was his brother.

In everyday life, distance blurs our sight. Having wrong ideas about people fogs our view. By not discerning the real person, we are misled, and, sadly, remain strangers. But if this fog lifts, we can learn to know each other and become friends. It is significant that in the Bible, one word expresses both 'to know' and 'to love'. Once we get to know each other, we are drawn together.

Cartographers of the Middle Ages had a strange practice. Whenever they were preparing a map and came across unknown territory, they filled the still-empty space with the picture of a wild beast. Unfortunately, people still mistrust and fear the unknown.

No wonder, therefore, that the ancient Greeks, ignorant of foreigners' language, explained their inability to understand what was being said by them not by admitting their own lack of knowledge, but by claiming that the foreigners were suffering from a speech impediment! Accordingly, they described them as 'stammerers'. The Greek word for this (and all it implies) survives in our word 'barbarians'.

Who finds a faithful friend, finds a treasure.

JEWISH SAYING

INFANCY TO
OLD AGE

F ROM INFANCY onwards we need to have and
make friends. Even babies still unable to speak will
stretch out their hands to touch each other or establish
eye contact — to gain a friend. And so it goes on
through all the stages of life, right up to its very end.
Naturally, the type of friendship changes and depends on
a great variety of factors. These include individual
economic and social circumstances, family background,
personal interests, one's psychological makeup and even
the environment. Some of the finest friendships may be
forged when sharing tribulations.

School friends

CHILDREN UNCONSCIOUSLY realise the necessity of
friendship. The sense of security it gives, the joyful
experience of belonging, are essential attributes of a
fulfilling life. Indeed, friendships play a paramount role
in the life of a child. They are responsible for countless
joys and, on occasion, they may also be the cause of
agonising disappointments.

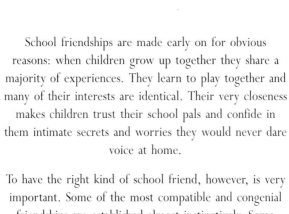

School friendships are made early on for obvious reasons: when children grow up together they share a majority of experiences. They learn to play together and many of their interests are identical. Their very closeness makes children trust their school pals and confide in them intimate secrets and worries they would never dare voice at home.

To have the right kind of school friend, however, is very important. Some of the most compatible and congenial friendships are established almost instinctively. Some unrealised affinity seems to attract one child to another. Nevertheless, it is wise for parents to keep an eye on their child's friendships. While never trying to choose their child's friends, or being unnecessarily interfering, they should watch over their child and try to help him or her avoid a wrong choice. A friendship can alter one's entire outlook and behaviour.

It has been shown that the way children make friends (or neglect to do so) is not merely of temporary significance. It may have a lasting influence on their adult personality and character and be at the root of traits which will one day determine their very place in society and their future achievements or problems.

School friendships may last a lifetime and often prove among the most rewarding, surviving even long periods of separation.

Adolescence to adulthood

FRIENDSHIP BECOMES the most relevant of all our relationships during adolescence, that period of crises, rebelliousness and uncertainty. To be able to share one's experiences and feelings with a friend can make all the difference at this awkward time. For instance, signs of puberty which may lead to a false sense of shame, social withdrawal or wrong types of 'experimentation' — with devastating results — can be freely discussed with one's peers.

Parents should play their part here, too. This is the very time when they must show that they are not only their child's father or mother, with wishes and opinions which should be respected, but that they are also real friends. Instead of adopting an outdated posture of authority, parents can try to guide and advise their children like equals. Parents should, after all, be able to bring memories of their own experience of the emotional and psychological turmoil of 'growing up' to their new friendship.

On the road of life

HAVING LEFT SCHOOL, new opportunities for friendship open up. We meet like-minded people with similar interests at college or university, or at a factory or office. Suddenly, a totally different aspect of 'grown-up' friendship is revealed to us, as we find special mates with whom we have so much to talk about.

Of course, having a boyfriend or a girlfriend at this time presents its own world of pleasures, demands and problems, depending on one's own maturity, sense of responsibility and expectations. A friendship based only on having a good time may not only quickly fade away, but may also spoil future happiness.

Once established in an occupation or profession, a busy schedule may leave the adult little time, making true friends all the more necessary and precious. After all, the depth of a friendship and its durability are what matter most, not the length of time we spend with a friend.

In a fulfilling marriage, one's spouse ought to be one's best friend, adding to love all the qualities which friendship offers. This does not mean, however, that we have to dispense with former friends. In some marriages a problem can arise when one of the partners resents or disapproves of the spouse's premarital friends. To just cut off such unwanted friends so as to avoid an argument would not only show lack of tolerance but also could prove a source of future disagreement. If you encounter such a situation, you should openly discuss it with your partner, aiming to come to a reasonable and amicable decision which hurts no one. To be fair, there will be instances where some former friends, being totally incompatible with one of the partners, may have to be discarded.

Old age

BY WHATEVER NAME it is known old age is nonetheless an inescapable chronological fact. Many of your former friends may have passed away, and the circle of people you can exchange visits with, and share memories, problems and worries with, becomes ever smaller. Feelings of being forgotten or 'left out' may play havoc. Loneliness may change what should be a beautiful evening of serenity before the setting of the sun into a dismal sequence of dragging hours, waiting for the night to come. Such a situation is often made worse by infirmity and the various deteriorations associated with ageing.

Two things are all-important. One, make every effort to keep old friendships 'in good repair'. Avoid any falling out with former friends. Be aware that it is easy to become intolerant of some human weaknesses they may have developed, and that a trivial occurrence can quickly assume a magnitude out of all proportion. Two, the young should be encouraged to extend their friendship to the old, not in a patronising way, but with genuine interest and affection. Simple little everyday attentions will be greatly appreciated by an older person as a way of 'keeping in touch', while the younger one will benefit from learning of things only the elderly know. If they are lucky, these young people one day will become 'senior citizens' too, and realise again the value of such cross-age friendships.

No man is useless while he has a friend.

ROBERT LOUIS STEVENSON

HOW TO
MAKE FRIENDS

Some friendships develop quite unexpectedly.
It is as though two minds meet and are attracted
to each other without forethought, as pins are attracted to
a magnet, only then to discover how much they have in
common. They are two halves destined for one another,
as it were, and join to become an inseparable one.

You may be fortunate to have made such a find already.
And somewhere, right now, new friends are waiting for
you to discover them, too. You can find them by
knowing how to make friends. Friendship is contagious
— but don't expect to catch it from others. Give them
an opportunity to catch it from *you*. Being friendly must
not be confused with being a friend. Above all,
remember that you cannot buy a friend!

Here are some of the many and diverse ways to make
and be a friend:

❖ *Be a caring person and give your heart. Friendship
is a caring and sharing relationship.*

❖ *Be sincere.*

❖ *Treat a person in the manner you want to be
treated yourself; be respectful.*

❖ *Be a good listener.*

❖ *Do not look for a perfect friend. No human is
without some fault.*

❖ *Do not expect to take more out of a friendship than you give to it.*

❖ *Realise that friendship is a dialogue, not a monologue.*

❖ *Never start a friendship for an end's sake. It won't last.*

❖ *Be cheerful.*

❖ *Give 'no strings attached' service; never be prompted by expectations of personal gain or advancement.*

❖ *Never pretend to be something you are not.*

❖ *Never try to impress those whom you want to become your friends.*

❖ *Above all, remember that in friendship it is not just a part of you that you offer: your reason, your feelings or some gift. It must be the whole of you.*

❖ *Friendship must be unqualified and unconditional. It must last 'through thick and thin'.*

❖ *You must trust your friend implicitly. At no time should you ever doubt your friend's word.*

❖ *Friendship demands complete openness. Nothing must be held back. To keep a secret from your friend is a vote of no confidence.*

A man who made friends
in an unusual way

THIS IS THE story of an extraordinary (but real) Mr Smith, a man well worth emulating. Without really planning it, he acquired many friends in a most unusual way.

It all started by accident. One day, he had a sudden idea about how a particular travel agency could increase its business through a novel type of advertisement. Oddly, he himself had no connection with the travel industry. He contacted the firm anyway and outlined his proposition, at the same time assuring them that should they adopt it, he would not expect any remuneration.

Shortly afterwards he received a letter of thanks informing him that the firm was about to implement his suggestion. Indeed, posters soon appeared around town as the result of his recommendation.

It all made him feel good and proud. Money could not have bought his sense of achievement. Probably the greatest reward was that the recipient of his advice became a life-long friend.

Having succeeded once, the practice of passing on helpful ideas became almost an addiction with Mr Smith. Whenever a flash of inspiration came to him, he would pass it on to the company or people who could benefit from it — and they were many and varied. For instance, he suggested to large stores how to improve the display of their goods. Religious communities also gained from his imaginative mind, his ideas enabling them to raise much-needed funds. If he came across items in

newspapers or magazines which he felt could be of assistance to a specific person or organisation, he would cut them out and pass them on to the parties concerned.

Mr Smith continued to give his ideas and 'finds' away — free of charge — for many years, well aware that he could often have sold them for a tidy profit. Still he was already making a good living and no money could have bought the friendships he made. And, the more ideas that came to him, the larger his circle of friends grew.

It is well worth adopting Mr Smith's practice. Apart from acquiring a treasure trove of most unexpected friends, it will keep your mind alert, active and young.

A man by himself is only half himself, for his friends are the other half; they reflect his soul as in a mirror.

Changing an enemy into a friend

THE BEST WAY to get rid of enemies is to make them into friends! However absurd this idea may sound at first, it is not an impossible task. You will need imagination, determination and perseverance, but, as you will find, it is well worth the effort.

Such metamorphoses have been achieved in the most trying circumstances. A typical example is that of an American clergyman who lived during the War of Independence. At the time, he was a most popular preacher and he had a host of friends, not least of whom was George Washington himself.

Nevertheless, he had made one enemy, a man who constantly tried to besmirch his name. This man was friendless himself, so the reason for his hostility was pure jealousy. Then one day, this individual was denounced as a traitor. He was tried for high treason, found guilty and sentenced to death.

The minister was determined to save the man's life. Only the President could stay an execution order, so he decided to call on the President — but to do so presented great difficulties. The President lived almost 100 kilometres away and the minister, being a person of few means, had no transport at his disposal. But this did not stop him: he walked all the way.

His mission seemed a failure. Though the President listened sympathetically to his plea, he was unbending. Justice had to take its course, he said, however much he would have liked to help save the minister's friend.

'Did you call him my friend?' the minister asked. 'Indeed, he is my worst enemy, but I can forgive him and so turn him into a friend.'

Washington was taken aback. He was amazed that anyone should walk all that distance to save an enemy. Deeply moved, he now pardoned the condemned man who subsequently changed in character and, though once the clergyman's relentless foe, went on to become his staunch friend.

One enemy is one too many.

Make books your friends

NO ONE NEED lack friends. In fact, a wealth of possible friends is waiting for you, right at this very moment. Take your pick! Once you have acquired these special friends, they will be yours forever. You will treasure them, and they will accompany you anywhere you go. They are books.

To make books your friends, select those you like best and love to keep. Soon they will be your constant companions. You may pick them up from your bedside table to reread just a few of their pages before turning out the light. Or, if you are plagued by a sleepless night, instead of tossing and turning, let a book help you pass the hours.

You may like to put one into your pocket and carry it with you. When waiting for a bus or train, or lining up in a queue, you will not be wasting precious time just standing and staring. By taking out your 'friend' and reading your favourite passages, you will fill empty moments with lasting value, deepen your knowledge and set your mind thinking. Books may help you take a break from the worries and anxieties of everyday life.

A book does not mind what you do with it. You may underline passages, annotate paragraphs with your own thoughts or earmark its pages. This friend will not resent any of this treatment but will become all the more treasured because of it. Note down the occasion when you first acquired your book on the title page, so you may recall it in years to come.

A book can prove a wonderful friend. Patiently waiting to be opened whenever you choose, it will provide you with food for thought, entertainment and enrichment. Nor will this friendship ever end, because you never really finish reading a book — on perusing it again, some thoughts which previously escaped you will suddenly strike you.

If you make a book your friend, you will never feel lonely, bored or lost. And, if you so desire, you will be able to hold communion with some of the greatest minds that have ever existed, and so be in the best of company.

When the Nazis occupied Holland in June 1942, Anne Frank had to go into hiding. She became isolated from all her friends so she made her diary her friend, even giving it a name — Kitty.

A book is a garden carried in the pocket.

ARAB PROVERB

Friendship on display

VISITS TO ART galleries may be very tiring and certainly do not appeal to everyone. It is there, however, that you may find the most unexpected friends — the exhibits themselves.

Walk slowly through the various halls and scan the paintings and sculptures till one of them reaches out for your attention. Stop there. Absorb all you find in it without trying to analyse what attracted you. Just keep looking at it, and you will have made a friend!

Don't go any further. You have seen enough. On your next visit, ignore all the other paintings and make your way straight to your newly-acquired friend. This time, you will discover many details and features which escaped you previously, and you will have grown so much closer.

Then continue your stroll till another exhibit or picture takes your fancy. Repeat the process — and you will have made yet another friend.

On each subsequent visit you can look forward to renewing your friendships and to being rewarded by discovering more beauty and meaning. Ultimately, you will eagerly anticipate meeting your old friends again. For you, going to the art gallery will not be merely an aesthetic pleasure, but a silent communion with precious friends who are always waiting for you.

A friend is a present you give yourself.

ROBERT LOUIS STEVENSON

The proper office of a friend is to side with you when you are in the wrong. Nearly anybody will side with you when you are in the right.

MARK TWAIN — NOTEBOOK

STORIES
OF FRIENDSHIP

Words to a mother-in-law

'. . . INTREAT ME NOT to leave you or to return from
following you: for where you go I will go; and where you
lodge, I will lodge: your people shall be my people, and
your God my God: where you die, will I die, and there
will I be buried: may the Lord do so to me, and more
also, even if death parts me from you.'

These words from the Book of Ruth, unsurpassed in
beauty, are known all over the western world. They are
frequently quoted or sung on occasions of supreme
happiness, such as wedding ceremonies, being thought to
express the love between a man and a woman.

Oddly, though, this belief is erroneous. When Ruth
uttered these words she did so not to her lover, but to (of
all people!) her mother-in-law! This is indeed intriguing,
given that mothers-in-law have rarely been the object of
friendship. They are more usually the butt of jokes.

Anthropologists have traced this peculiar attitude to a
taboo that obsessed primitive societies, the ritual
practice of 'mother-in-law avoidance'. They believed that
one's mother-in-law presented an ominous threat to be
escaped from. Thus they not only avoided her company,
but even steered clear of catching a casual glimpse of
her. Mother-in-law avoidance became so deeply rooted

in the human consciousness that it still survives as a sort of ancestral memory, greatly accounting for the modern phenomenon of mother-in-law aversion. This portrayal of the once fond bond between a mother-in-law and her daughter-in-law, these words of most affectionate friendship as voiced by Ruth, are therefore all the more significant.

'I knew you would come!'

TRUE FRIENDSHIP KNOWS no limits, no matter what the cost. Friends' trust in each other can sustain them in even the most trying situations. They can rely on each other's word and promise, however much circumstances seem to speak against their fulfilment.

Once there was a man wrongly condemned to death for a crime he had not committed. He was denied the opportunity to prove his innocence and was locked away to await execution. His best friend was convinced that the man was not guilty, so he approached the authorities and offered to take the prisoner's place, thus enabling his friend to find the real perpetrator of the crime. This was agreed upon with the understanding that, should his friend fail to return, he would be put to death in his stead.

The date set for the execution came ever closer, without a word from the accused. People began to taunt the loyal prisoner that his friend would not return at all, and he would have to die on the gallows — but nothing could shake the fellow's belief that this would not happen.

On the appointed day, there was still no news. The crowds had already gathered to watch the gruesome spectacle, with even the king being present. The final hours passed and the dreadful moment came. The friend was taken to the place of execution, with only minutes separating him from death . . .

Meanwhile, the accused had succeeded in finding the real culprit. However, on his way back to the prison, a storm had come up and delayed him considerably. He realised what any delay on his part would mean, so with superhuman effort, straining every muscle almost beyond endurance, he sped on to make up for lost time. His exertions were not in vain. He arrived at the very instant his friend was mounting the steps to the scaffold. On seeing him, the friend called out, 'I knew you would come!'

Physically and emotionally exhausted, the two embraced each other. Deeply touched by this spectacle of a friendship that had known no bounds, the king immediately released the prisoner and greatly rewarded both men.

Greater love hath no man than this, that a man lay down his life for his friends.

JOHN 15, 13

All for one, one for all

THE SCOPE OF friendship goes beyond the relationship between just two people. It can extend to an entire group of friends whose determination to help each other can overcome obstacles and predicaments which they could never tackle individually. The range of such situations is wide, including people's survival together in a hostile environment, or during times of ethnic, racial or religious persecution, or through grave financial difficulties. There is no lack of historical examples. The role of friendship in such circumstances has been aptly summarised by the famous motto in Dumas' *The Three Musketeers* — 'All for one, one for all.' The fable that follows speaks of this motto's successful application in the animal world.

A goat, a rat, a tortoise and a raven made up a most unlikely assortment of friends, but they met regularly and enjoyed each other's company. When one day the goat did not turn up, something most unusual on her part, her friends became worried that something untoward must have happened to her.

They decided the raven should fly over the entire area in search of their missing pal. It was not long before he spotted the goat. She had been caught in a hunter's net from which she was unsuccessfully trying to disentangle herself.

There was no doubt in the animals' minds that they had to go to her rescue. The rat immediately volunteered to be carried by the raven to the site of the trap. There, with his sharp teeth, he would gnaw through the net and liberate their friend. By acting jointly and losing no

time, the three achieved their rescue mission. Just when
they were about to depart, their fourth companion,
the slow tortoise, arrived.

'Oh, friend', cried the goat, 'Why did you come? Any
moment now the hunter may be here and how can you
ever escape from him at your pace?'

The tortoise was about to say that she could not enjoy
safety while her friend's life was in danger when, as
feared, the hunter arrived.

The goat was able to rush off, the raven flew away
and the rat quickly disappeared into a hole. The tortoise,
however, could only crawl off — with the result that she
had covered hardly any distance when the hunter caught
her and put her in his bag, in anticipation
of a good evening meal.

The three friends saw what had happened and were
determined not to abandon the tortoise. By joint action
they would set her free. The goat left her hiding place
and shammed a bad limp to appear an easy prey. The
ruse worked. The hunter caught sight of her and started
in pursuit. To be able to run faster, he threw down the
bag containing the tortoise. This gave the others a
chance to free their friend. The moment they had done
so, the goat, no longer limping, ran away to freedom,
as did her three friends.

*We are born for cooperation, as are the feet, the
hands, the eyelids, and the upper and lower jaws.*

MARCUS AURELIUS, MEDITATIONS

A Hindu legend

INDRA, ONE OF the chief Hindu deities, was visiting a forest close to the city of Benares. He thought he had rarely — even in his heavenly abode — encountered anything as beautiful as the exquisite foliage and majestic growth he found there.

While he was walking through the wood, Indra's attention was suddenly drawn to a withered tree. It was totally decayed and had lost all its leaves. However, surprisingly, a bird was perched on one of the bare branches.

'How silly you are to sit on a dead tree! All around you the trees are full of leaves,' scoffed Indra.

'That may be so', replied the bird. 'But, you see, the nest in which I was born was in this very tree. From its boughs I learnt to fly and its foliage gave me shelter. Should I desert this tree now that it is old and has lost its lush growth? It has been my friend throughout my life and it would be most ungrateful of me to forsake it just because age has withered it.'

Indra was deeply impressed by the bird's words and remarked, 'If only humans showed equal compassion and gratitude to their friends!' He then promised to grant the bird any special wish in recognition of its loyal friendship.

'All I want', said the bird, 'is for you to restore this tree to its former glory.'

Indra lost no time in doing so.

Fortunate indeed are those who experience a friendship as loyal and long-lasting as that of this legendary Indian

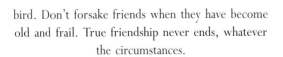

bird. Don't forsake friends when they have become old and frail. True friendship never ends, whatever the circumstances.

Such persistence should apply to our relationships with our pets. Pets grow old and become infirm too; they may become arthritic or lethargic, and are no longer able to amuse us as they once did, no matter how much they would like to. To discard them would be a poor reward for their friendship and for the many hours of happiness their company and affection gave us.

We must be friends — always!

A friend loves at all times.

PROVERBS 17, 17

Heaven and hell

FORGETTING ONE'S OWN needs while showing concern
for another's welfare is a distinguishing mark of
friendship. This imaginative interpretation of the concepts
of heaven and hell provides a striking illustration.

A man was granted a glimpse into life after death in a
dream. It reflected the ancient belief in the existence
of both a heavenly kingdom of celestial bliss, reserved
for the meritorious, and a place of torment set
aside for the damned.

First, he was taken to hell. He was amazed to find there
a large banqueting table laden with every type of
delicacy. A plaque on the wall stipulated that those who
wanted to partake of the food were obliged to use the
knives, forks and spoons that had been specially supplied.
He also noticed that these had such long handles that no
one was able to get the food into their mouth.
Consequently, the people were starving to death.

He was then shown heaven. Surprisingly, its arrangement
was identical with what he had encountered in hell.
There was the same sort of table with all the delicious
fare and the plaque demanding exclusive use of the long-
handled cutlery. But no one was starving, because they
were feeding each other!
They were all friends.

**Dostoevski defined hell as the suffering
of being unable to love.**

The tale of an axe

IT IS EASY to join in when people are having fun. A true test of genuine friendship, however, is when things go wrong. This simple tale dramatically makes this point.

Two friends were walking across a field and came across an axe lying on the ground. One immediately picked it up, informing his friend that he would sell it.

'I've found it', he claimed, 'and so I shall enjoy the money.'

'That is not correct', protested the other. 'We spotted it together and so it is only proper for us to split the proceeds.'

But his companion vehemently refused to do so. He was determined to be the only one to profit from their joint find. The two had not gone much further when they met a farmer who immediately recognised the axe as being his. He went to claim his property, accusing the man carrying it of having stolen the axe.

'We are certainly in trouble now', remarked the sham friend to his companion.

'Not at all', replied the latter. '*We* are not in trouble — *you* are! A little while ago you rejected our common claim to the axe. How can you now expect me to share your trouble?'

A small boy was asked to describe a friend. His immediate reply was, 'He is someone who sticks to you after he has found you out.'

Friends who drop us

OCCASIONALLY IT HAPPENS that someone whom we have always considered a friend suddenly, and for no apparent reason, drops us.

Of course, there is usually an explanation. Friendship is much too precious to just let go. We ought to try to seek out the cause of any such fracture and act accordingly.

No one is blameless. At some time or other it is likely that we will do or say things that, in retrospect, we will regret. It may be that, unintentionally or even unknowingly, we have hurt our friend, who is too upset to discuss the matter, and avoids or abandons us.

Recall your past friendship, making every effort to ascertain whether perhaps the rift was brought about by some thoughtless action on your part. However difficult it might seem, call on your former friend and, speaking freely, try to resolve your differences. It will certainly not cheapen you to say, 'I'm sorry!' and it may well result in a renewal of your friendship, none the worse for the crisis.

Severance of relations need not be permanent. When you are emotionally drained, or exasperated, in the heat of the moment, you may have parted vowing never to see each other again. Let some time pass. When your tempers have cooled, you might see things differently. Perhaps one or both of you were under great stress at the time. Don't wait for the other party to make the first move either. Take the initiative and have the courage to admit when you have been wrong or have exaggerated an issue.

Sometimes jealousy may be at the root of a sudden alienation. Less fortunate friends may resent your success or happy marriage, or some other thing which has so far eluded them. There are, unfortunately, some people whose attitude to their friends is influenced mainly by success — theirs or their friends'. Another possibility is that a third party has poisoned your friendship, also motivated by jealousy. In either case, any efforts to re-establish the lost friendship would be wasted. An envious person can never be a true friend; nor can someone who listens to mischievous gossip.

Rarer, but not any less hurtful, is the friend who simply no longer wants to know you, or who even goes to the extreme of becoming your outright antagonist. This is a documented psychological phenomenon, usually stemming from some long-forgotten incident where the friend was in distress and you were able to help resolve the problem. Some people want to forget all about such past favours and do not wish to be reminded of their former state of need or dependence.

Even Abraham Lincoln was aware of this quirky human failing, having been a victim of it himself. When one of his friends not only refused to support him on a vital issue but showed vehement and unreasonable hostility, he remarked, 'I cannot understand why this man has become my enemy, I cannot remember ever doing him a favour!'

'Friends' of this kind are not worth having. In fact, don't be distressed if they drop you. Put them out of your life and mind. In some cases, those who stop being your friend were never real friends to begin with.

Be realistic as well. People change. Gradually, though not very noticeably at first, friends might drift apart. They outgrow their once most intimate relationship and are simply no longer compatible. This is a fact of life. Remember that to force the continuation of a friendship that has become meaningless is futile.

A doubtful friend is worse than a certain enemy.

AESOP

A friend is one who knows all about you and loves you all the same.

You can mend a broken vase, but the crack is still there.

HUNGARIAN PROVERB

A toast to absent friends

WHEN CELEBRATING A happy occasion it is customary to include among the toasts one to 'absent friends'. This is no mere formality, as it provides an opportunity to reflect on the value of friends. We can think fondly of them even if they are unable to be with us. No matter how far away they might be, we know that they are with us in spirit, and that they are joining in our happiness.

Two frequently-quoted and somewhat contradictory proverbs claim that 'absence makes the heart grow fonder' and that 'out of sight is out of mind'. Neither of them applies to real friendship, which does not lessen or grow by separation. It is unchanging. Friends are for keeps and even though we may not have seen them for a prolonged period of time, nothing will influence the intensity of our relationship, our concern and our commitment.

Never take friendship for granted. Just as in any other close relationship, it is good to regularly reaffirm its importance. This is all the more essential in our hectic present-day world with its tight schedules and numerous stresses. We have little time for ourselves and our families, let alone our friends.

A friendship day

WHY NOT SET aside one day every year as a 'friendship day'? It could be a public holiday, or a day which has special personal significance. Reserve it just for your friends. How you use your 'friendship day' is up to you. Perhaps you might phone friends if they live nearby and update each other on what has happened since you last communicated. For friends who are further away, you could write a letter, fax a message, send flowers or some other token of friendship. Your friends will appreciate that you are thinking of them and you will feel better for it, too.

Mark Twain once wisely remarked that unless people kept painting a white fence, time and again, it would go grey. The principle also applies to friendship.

The Lord watch between you and me, when we are absent one from the other.

GENESIS 31, 49

HISTORIC FRIENDSHIPS

IT HAS NOT always been realised how history and civilisation owe some notable advances and achievements to the close friendship of two individuals, and of how their mutual help, encouragement and inspiration enriched humanity.

All the more surprising is the fact that some of those creative associations have been all but forgotten or, in some cases, credit has only been given to one party. Here are some interesting examples of such historic friendships

David and Jonathan

MANY GENERATIONS HAVE found inspiration in the Biblical account of the friendship between young David and Jonathan. It was said of them that their souls were knit together in an inseparable bond (I Samuel 18, 1). No clash of loyalties could break up their friendship. The elegy in which David voiced his grief on hearing of Jonathan's tragic death and passionately recalled their friendship, which could not be surpassed even by the love of a woman, is a classic tribute to friendship.

Bass and Flinders

THE HISTORY OF Australia's exploration owes much to the friendship of Matthew Flinders and George Bass. Flinders, who was responsible for the adoption of the name 'Australia' was one of the world's most outstanding navigators at that time. Bass was a naval surgeon who shared Flinders' passion for discovery.

They served together on the frigate HMS *Reliance*, Flinders as midshipman and Bass as surgeon. In 1795, they sailed from Britain for the 'great southern land' and the then fledgling settlement of Port Jackson. The two were to become the closest of friends, and jointly undertook several history-making surveys and expeditions.

In his *Voyage* to *Terra Australis*, Flinders recalled, 'In George Bass I had the happiness to find a man whose ardour for discovery was not to be repressed by any obstacles nor deterred by any danger, and with this friend a determination was formed of completing the examination of the east coast of New South Wales . . .'

These two friends' achievements live on in perpetuity in the map of Australia — Bass Strait and the Flinders Ranges.

Watt and Boulton

IT IS NOT COMMONLY known that James Watt's development of the steam engine would have been impossible without the help of his friend, Matthew Boulton. Their partnership started in 1775 and extended over a period of 25 years.

In 1781 it was Boulton who encouraged Watt to invent the all-important rotary motion for the engine. When lack of money prevented Watt from proceeding with his history-making work, it was Boulton who provided the necessary financial support.

The consequence of these two men's friendship is incalculable indeed. Their close bond helped to pioneer modern automation and so was, in no small measure, responsible for the Industrial Revolution. It is therefore regrettable that, generally, Watt alone is given the credit and remembered as the inventor of the steam engine. It was with Boulton's help that Watt originated the term 'horsepower'. Still, to this day, we honour Watt alone, even calling the appropriate unit of power in the metric system after him — the kilowatt.

Some friendships grow simply out of shared interests and pursuits. Though a pair might be mere companions at first, close cooperation and having to jointly face problems, work and even dangers can result in an inseparable union. This was so in the little-known case of Watt and Boulton.

Goethe and Schiller

JOHANN WOLFGANG VON GOETHE and Friedrich von Schiller were Germany's foremost dramatists and poets. The former is renowned for his *Faust* and the other for his *Ode to Joy*, which provided the text for the last movement of Beethoven's *Ninth Symphony*. Though Goethe is now recognised as probably being the greater of the two, their contemporaries argued as to which was the more gifted.

Both men resided in Weimar, and from 1794 onwards they became close friends, stimulating each other's literary creativity. Together they denounced mediocrity and fought for a nobler society. They met frequently and admired each other's qualities, each ranking the other above himself. When people complimented one as being the superior writer he would vehemently reject the praise as being unjustified.

To commemorate their unique literary friendship, the city of Weimar erected a monument in the middle of the 19th century. This is a very unusual sculpture which ingeniously depicts their mutual appreciation. Goethe is shown holding a laurel wreath with which he is about to crown his friend. Schiller, however, is refusing the honour in favour of his friend. The sculpture dramatically expresses the very moment when neither of them will accept the wreath, each offering it to the other.

Byron and Shelley

THE FRIENDSHIP BETWEEN Percy Bysshe Shelley and Lord Byron, both regarded in their day as the greatest English poets, was well known. It is also significant that Byron's name was coupled with that of Goethe as being among the leading creative spirits of the time.

Shelley and Byron had much in common and their lives shared many features. Both were educated in Public Schools, they both had marriages which broke up and both enjoyed a lifestyle which openly defied the mores of the period. Ostracised by English society, they went to live abroad.

Byron was introduced to Shelley by Claire, Mary Shelley's stepsister, who later became Byron's mistress and mother of his daughter Allegra. The two men became instant friends: like Goethe and Schiller, they enjoyed each other's company and provided great intellectual stimulation for each other.

Their friendship was to continue for six years. It was cut short in 1822 by Shelley's sudden death in a drowning accident, at the age of 29. The many similarities in their lives seemed to continue to the very end. Byron was to die a relatively young man, too, as a result of rheumatic fever — at the age of 36.

Boswell and Johnson

THE MOST UNLIKELY friendship developed between the Scottish-born James Boswell and the English author Samuel Johnson. They first met in 1763 in a London bookstore. Johnson was then 54 years old and Boswell 23, young enough to be Johnson's son.

When Boswell first visited Johnson, he did so uninvited. There must have somehow been an immediate rapport, as on parting Johnson asked him to come again. From then onward they spent a great deal of time together.

On Boswell's departure for the Netherlands, Johnson came to see him off. Their friendship became even firmer on his return. Boswell took copious notes of their conversations, and these formed the basis of his famous biography of his friend, the creator of the history-making *Dictionary of Samuel Johnson*.

Ten years after their first meeting, Johnson accompanied Boswell on a tour of the Scottish Highlands and the Hebrides, with the great enjoyment on the part of both friends being noted by contemporaries.

Boswell was devastated by Johnson's death. When he saw and spoke to his friend in a dream, he asked Johnson to pray to God that they would be granted the opportunity of meeting again. Soon afterwards Boswell embarked on his *Life of Samuel Johnson*, the work which was to immortalise both friends.

It is intriguing to learn that one of Johnson's most notable contributions to *The Gentleman's Magazine*, for which he wrote regularly, was a poem called "Friendship."

Roosevelt and Hopkins

PRESIDENT FRANKLIN D. ROOSEVELT's association with Harry Hopkins is an example of enduring friendship in modern times.

It is very rare for people in top positions to have real friends. They are more usually destined to lead lonely existences, for the majority of so-called friends turn out to be mere opportunists and sycophants.

However, all Hopkins wanted out of his friendship with the President was the gratifying knowledge that he could be of service. He even lived in the White House for some time, using a simple card table in his bedroom as a writing desk.

Harry became Roosevelt's confidant and frequent advisor. He had a passion for social justice, sound common sense and a practical mind, which proved of vital importance during some of the worst crises of the Second World War. It has even been said that Hopkins played a considerable part in bringing the war to its successful conclusion.

When asked about their unique relationship, Roosevelt confessed that, as the President of the United States, he could look at the door leading into his office and know that practically everyone walking through it wanted something out of him. Harry Hopkins, on the other hand, asked for nothing.

The two men's friendship was not confined to matters of state or world politics: it also embraced their private pursuits. A true friendship indeed, which lasted to the very end.

ANIMAL PALS

T HOUGH IT IS denied by some authorities, the phenomenon of friendship may even exist between animals and, surprisingly, not only among their own kind.

For instance, some horses seem to be inseparable and a 'friend's' absence can be most upsetting to them. It has been observed that a goat has a calming effect on a highly strung horse.

Elephants are renowned for their affectionate friendship towards each other, shown not least in the care they extend to members of their group who are old and sick. Dolphins are well known for their intelligence, and appear to excel in acts of friendship as well. They have been observed giving extraordinary support to an injured companion, holding it up to the surface to inhale the air that is essential for its survival. Even the mutual grooming observed between baboons has been explained, at least in part, as an expression of affectionate friendship.

The show of friendship discovered between vampire bats who nightly feed on the blood of cattle is most astounding. If a bat fails to obtain a meal for two consecutive nights, it is sure to die. Well aware of its imminent fate, such a bat will approach one of its mates in the hope of sharing some of the blood this one has drunk. In most instances, the call for help will not go unanswered. The fellow bat will regurgitate some of its meal to save the other's life. An immediate bond is then forged between the donor and the recipient. Should a reciprocal favour be required at any time in the future, the original recipient will assist its friend. It is intriguing that this animal, so generally repugnant to people, so excels at friendship, manifested in this selfless act of saving a friend from certain death by starvation.

The unique bond of friendship experienced between an animal and a human, both in war and peace, is inspiring indeed. All the technology of our present day society cannot replace such relationships, which are expressed in so many ways. Moving examples are the devotion of the 'seeing eye' and 'hearing ear' dogs.

General Eisenhower gratefully acknowledged what the friendship of his dog meant to him in far-off Africa: 'The friendship of a dog is precious. It becomes even more so when one is so far removed from home as we are in Africa. I have a Scottie. In him I find consolation and diversion . . . He is the one "person" to whom I can talk without conversation coming back to the war.'

At an early period of his life, young Lord Byron regarded his black and white Newfoundland dog Boatswain as his 'only friend'. He was deeply grieved at its death, and had Boatswain laid to rest in the grounds of Newstead Abbey, the Byrons' ancestral home. At the time he even expressed the wish that, on his own passing, his ashes should be buried next to Boatswain, 'my faithful dog, whose body should never be removed from the vault'. Byron had a monument erected, inscribed with an epitaph he wrote in memory of his canine friend:

Near this Spot
are deposited the Remains of one
who possessed Beauty without Vanity,
Strength without Insolence,
Courage without Ferocity,
and all the Virtues of Man without his Vices.
This Praise, which would be unmeaning Flattery
if inscribed over human Ashes,
is but a just tribute to the Memory of

BOATSWAIN, A DOG

who was born in Newfoundland May 1802
and died at Newstead. Nov. 18th 1808.

The friendship between an animal and a human is especially moving. It is a relationship which extends beyond the death of either the animal or its 'master'.

Many of us have experienced friendship with an animal or known some wonderful examples. Such friendships can enrich lives, make lonely people happy, give solace in sorrow, ease the pain of the bedridden and, in not a few cases, even save the human friend's life. Modern science has confirmed that an attachment to a pet can greatly contribute to a person's wellbeing. It can lower elevated blood pressure, and soothe the mind of a troubled patient.

Animals are such agreeable friends; they ask no
questions, they pass no criticism.

GEORGE ELIOT

'Greyfriar's Bobby'

A FOUNTAIN NEAR Greyfriar's Church in Edinburgh, Scotland, is topped with a statue of a little terrier dog named Bobby. He has become so famous that people refer to him as 'Greyfriar's Bobby'.

Bobby was a dog who belonged to a shepherd named Jock Gray. The two were inseparable friends. When his master died in 1858 and was buried in Greyfriar's churchyard, the faithful little dog's friendship did not cease. For 14 years he sat on Jock's grave, guarding it. He never left it. Had it not been for the people of Edinburgh who fed him, Bobby would have starved to death.

In recognition of Bobby's unswerving loyalty, the city of Edinburgh adopted him. When he died too, after many years, he was buried next to his beloved master and immortalised by the statue.

How a dog inspired a proverb

FAR AWAY IN Tokyo, another statue also commemorates a canine friendship. This one is made of bronze and stands in front of Shibuya station, where it has become a favourite meeting place.

Professor Ueno, who taught at Tokyo University in the 1920s, received a puppy for a gift. Hachi, as he named it, was a mischievous little dog who soon endeared

himself to the entire neighbourhood. People referred to him affectionately as 'Hachi-ko' meaning 'Dear Hachi'.

To get to the university, Professor Ueno used to catch a train from Shibuya station. It did not take long for Hachi-ko to make it his practice to accompany the Professor to the station and see him off before trotting home. He would then return at 5.30 pm each evening to meet the train which brought his beloved master home again.

One day Hachi-ko was having his usual afternoon nap when he suddenly jumped up. Barking frantically, he dashed off madly to the station, many hours before the professor was due to arrive . . . but Hachi-ko waited in vain. The professor had suffered a fatal stroke — eerily, at the very moment Hachi-ko had woken up with such a start.

For many years afterwards Hachi-ko persisted in meeting the train regularly at 5.30 pm, obviously expecting his human friend who, alas, never came. He continued to do so till he himself passed away 10 years later. The little dog's loyalty and friendship so touched the hearts of the people of Shibuya that they erected the statue in his memory. Indeed, Hachi-ko's name has become part of a proverb to express any dog's devout and faithful friendship, *Chuuken Hachiko*.

Standing guard

A QUEENSLAND FARMER who was run over by his own
tractor lay on the ground for 11 days before being
rescued. During all that time his faithful dog Bimbo
stayed with him, fighting off the crows which almost
ceaselessly tried to attack the helpless man.

Canine know-how

Trixie was a six-year-old Kelpie cross and the constant
companion of Jack, a 75-year-old pensioner.
She was to save his life, too.

Jack lived all alone and, when he suffered a stroke, he
lay paralysed and helpless in bed at his Sydney home.
He was quite unable to move and could not even crawl
to the phone. However, Trixie sustained him for nine
days. Whenever Jack called for water, she would bring
it to him from her own bowl. She did so very cleverly,
by dipping a towel into the water and then draping it
over the prostrate man's face so he could suck at the
moisture. When no water was left in the dish, Trixie
found another source of supply — the toilet bowl.

Jack was eventually found by his family and taken to
hospital, where it took him five months to recover.
Doctors agreed that he owed his life to Trixie.

An animal blanket

IT WAS THE middle of winter in a remote part of New Zealand. Thick snow made the ground treacherous, causing a passing stockman to fall off his horse and break his leg. He would have frozen to death had his six dogs not covered him with their bodies to keep him warm. He was eventually spotted by a helicopter and help arrived. It was then found that one of the dogs, a labrador bitch, had actually given her life in this unique act of friendship. She had succumbed to the cold and her stiff body had to be lifted from across her master's.

Suzie, the bachelor's cat

ANIMAL PETS HAVE been known to drag a drowning person from the water and enter buildings enveloped in flames to save an adult or child from being burnt to death or choked by the smoke. Still, friendship between animals and humans works both ways, and numerous examples have also been recorded of people risking everything to save their four-legged friends.

For instance, there was a cat, Suzie, who belonged to an English bachelor named Frank. Suzie had been taken seriously ill with feline 'flu, which is mostly fatal. There seemed to be little hope of her surviving. Frank took off a week from work to nurse Suzie day and night — perhaps the oddest type of 'sick leave'. However, his efforts were rewarded and he saved Suzie's life. It is ironic that when he happily returned to work, he was sacked!

FAVOURITE POEMS AND PROVERBS

My old friend

ARTHUR CHRISTOPHER BENSON (1862–1925), a one-time Master of Magdalene College, Cambridge, England, wrote about a wide range of experiences, human tribulations and pleasures. Nothing gave him greater joy than writing. He compared it to the appetite of a famished person about to partake of a nourishing meal.

Benson was well aware of the blessings friendship could bestow, especially if extended to people deprived of those gifts we ordinarily take for granted. Benson provided specific examples. In every community — even in the smallest village — there is likely to be a cripple or blind person living in tragic isolation. To visit them is an act of generosity and friendship.

There is a wealth of possible friendships we can create in the least expected quarters. They will not remain one-sided, but will prove most rewarding. Benson's philosophy and thoughts make this poem all the more meaningful.

It seems that the world was always bright
With some divine unclouded weather
When we, with hearts and footsteps light,
By lawn and river walked together:

There was no talk of me and you,
    Of theories with facts to bound them,
We were content to be and do,
    And take our fortunes as we found them.

We spoke no wishful words of love,
    No hint of sympathy and dearness,
Only around, beneath, above,
    There ran a swift and subtle nearness.

Each inmost thought was known to each
    By some impetuous divination:
We found no need of flattering speech,
    Content with silent admiration.

I think I never touched your hand,
    I took no heed of face or feature,
Only, I thought on sea or land
    Was never such a gracious creature.

It seems I was not hard to please,
    Where'er you led I needs must follow;
For strength you were my Hercules,
    For wit and lustre my Apollo.

The years flew onward: stroke by stroke
    They clashed from the impartial steeple,
And we appear to other folk
    A pair of ordinary people.

One word, old friend: though fortune flies,
    If hope should fail, till death shall sever,
In one dim pair of faithful eyes
    You seem as bright, as brave as ever.

A. C. Benson

Friendship

I'd like to be the sort of friend that you
    have been to me,
I'd like to be the help that you are always
    glad to be.
I'd like to mean as much to you, each
    minute of the day,
As you have meant, old friend of mine, to
    me along the way.
I'd like to do the big things and the splendid
    things for you,
To brush the grey from out your skies and
    leave them only blue.
I'd like to say the kind of things that I so oft
    have heard,
And feel that I could rouse your soul the
    way that mine you stirred.
I'd like to give you back the joy that you
    have given me,
Yet that were wishing you a need I hope
    will never be.
I'd like to make you feel as rich, as I who
    travel on
Undaunted in the darkest hours, with you
    to lean upon.
I'm wishing at this very time that I could
    but repay
A portion of the gladness that you've strewn
    along my way.
And could I have one wish today, this only
    would it be . . .
I'd like to be the sort of friend that you have
    been to me

RUSS TYSON'S PHILOSOPHER'S NOTE BOOK

*What is offered in friendship must
not be weighed on a scale.*
CHINESE PROVERB

*Be conscientious in speaking to your friend, but
tactful in your efforts to guide him aright.*
CONFUCIUS

Hold a true friend with both your hands.
NIGERIAN PROVERB

*It is better to lose money with a friend
who is clever than with a fool.*
RUSSIAN PROVERB

*Do not protect yourself by a fence,
but rather by your friends.*
CZECH PROVERB

Give and take makes good friends.
SCOTTISH PROVERB

None is so rich as to throw away a friend.
TURKISH PROVERB

*He who seeks a faultless friend,
remains friendless.*
TURKISH PROVERB

Reckoning up is friendship's end.
IRISH PROVERB

It is good to have a friend even in hell.
SPANISH PROVERB

In times of trouble you know your friends.
IRISH PROVERB

*You can recognise a bird by its feathers
and a man by his friends.*
HUNGARIAN PROVERB

Symbols
of Friendship

Traditionally, the gesture of shaking hands
expresses and seals this treasured bond. Clasped hands
represent friends' close attachment. By firmly holding
each other, they serve as a mutual support.

Early on, salt was recognised and used as a preservative
to maintain the freshness of food. It is little wonder,
therefore, that it came to symbolise incorruptible
friendship which nothing could ever spoil.

In the language of flowers, many plants have been used
to highlight various aspects of friendship.

For instance, the clinging ivy was used to represent the
inseparable attachment of true friends. Ivy appears to
caress the object on which it grows and not even a
tempestuous storm can dislodge it.

Rosemary became a symbol of remembrance because of
its lingering scent, and also its assumed ability to aid
memory. Sir Thomas Moore had rosemary growing all
over his garden wall. He explained that this was '. . . not
only because my bees love it, but because it is the herb
sacred to remembrance, and therefore to friendship.'

Violets depicted with their blooms touching each other
had a special message: that, thus joined, their combined
scent would be stronger and spread further. Friendship
similarly affects not only the individuals concerned, but
it enriches the world around them.

A CHILD'S VIEW

HERE IS A COLLECTION of definitions and
thoughts on friendship from ordinary children.

❖ *Friends are people that play with you*
and care about you.

❖ *Friends are good for company. If you don't have friends*
you would be really bored.

❖ *I help my friend when he is crying to make*
him feel better.

❖ *Friends are people who care about you and*
people who don't tease you.

❖ *You can trust your friends on anything, but you have to make*
sure that they can trust you back. When you have a fight with
your friend it can be really heartbreaking, but you know
you will make up soon.

❖ *A friend is a person who shares and cares and is fun to be with.*
A friend will help you when you are down, phone you when you are
sick or away from school. If you need a lift home or you don't know
what a word or sum is, you can always ask a friend. If you are
thirsty or tired, hungry or injured, or you need a dollar to catch the
bus; for company, laughter and sharing of jokes, for advice or to
keep a secret you can always turn to a friend. It doesn't matter if
your friend is a girl or a boy, black or white, Jewish or Christian,
Greek or American, that person can be your friend.

❖ *Friendship is a bond between people that isn't based on one's*
looks but on what is beneath the skin. Not their appearance but
their personality is something that is very important to me and I
think it's important to many other people. If there was more
friendship among nations there would be fewer wars and racist
demonstrations. There would be no need for spies or weaponry. We
could depend on each other and not on weapons and stealing.

FRIENDSHIP — HOPE FOR OUR WORLD

NOW, MORE THAN at any time in our history, people from different backgrounds, cultures, races and religions must learn to respect each other and foster individual friendships. As a starting point, children should be taught — at home and in school — to abstain from ugly generalisations and from saying or doing anything that might belittle, harm or hurt other people.

Interfaith

Religion should serve as an example in promoting genuine friendship, and has started doing so with the establishment of the ecumenical movement and interfaith councils. There is no need to deny obvious distinctions which cannot be overcome — and variety is healthy in all things — but all faiths share essential fundamentals. The once-prevalent attitudes of self-righteousness which saw individual faiths each claiming to be the only 'true one', are outdated. The most we can claim is that to us personally, the religion to which we belong, by birth or by choice, is the most fulfilling.

A very telling apocryphal story may be told here, of a conversation between an Anglican primate and his Catholic cardinal friend. In pursuit of modern ecumenism, they had held a combined service of their denominations. It was a notable occasion and was attended by a vast congregation. Later, when they were discussing their success, both clergymen expressed their gratification.

'How wonderful for us to combine in worshipping God', one said to the other. His colleague responded, 'Yes, you in your way and I in His.'

Unfortunately, this is the very attitude which still survives among some narrow-minded people and which we must discard. Only by becoming personal friends and learning to differentiate between what is irrelevant and what is essential will we realise how much we can learn from and give to each other.

Overcoming prejudice

In many parts of the world, races and nations who once kept themselves strictly apart now mix freely. In spite of the unmistakable survival of some racial and ethnic hatreds and prejudices, there is a steadily growing number of people who now ask not who you are, but what sort of person you are. Just as in the realm of religion, personal friendships between those of diverse ethnic, racial and social backgrounds have assumed paramount importance. After all, there is only *one* humanity.

However, as Blake once warned, to speak only in generalities is gross hypocrisy. It is individual action that matters. We must each go out of our way to make friends with those who come from different races, countries or social environments. To establish such relationships has become one of the great challenges we each face, whoever we are and wherever we live.

A political point

A MINOR AND yet significant tradition is followed in the Westminster system of democracy. After the maiden speech from a new Member of Parliament, he or she is congratulated not by a representative of their own party, but by a Member of the Opposition!

To sit on opposite sides, literally or metaphorically, and passionately express conflicting views should not necessarily create antagonism. Instead of denigrating one another, political opponents should foster personal friendships and recognise that it is the very diversity of their opinion which helps to build a strong nation and happier society.

Friendship week

A VALUABLE AID in breaking down all man-made barriers to friendship would be to institute, both nationally and internationally, an annual friendship week.

This could be fostered jointly by various religious bodies, government agencies, unions, municipal councils, service clubs, sporting organisations and, not least, the media. Every school could make it a major annual project. Ideas and activities for a friendship week could pave the way for world harmony, for friendship, indeed, is the hope of our world.

Without confidence there is no friendship.

EPICURUS

Thank you for being my friend